THE DEAD BOY SINGS IN HEAVEN

THE DEAD BOY SINGS IN HEAVEN

LANA HECHTMAN AYERS

NIGHT RAIN PRESS

Copyright © 2018 Lana Hechtman Ayers

http://LanaAyers.com

All rights reserved. No part of this publication may be reproduced, distributed, or transmitted in any form or by any means whatsoever without written permission from the publisher, except in the case of brief excerpts for critical reviews and articles. All inquiries should be addressed to Night.Rain.Press@gmail.com.

FIRST EDITION

Printed in the United States of America

ISBN: 978-0-9970834-9-1

Cataloging Information: 1. Ayers, Lana Hechtman; 2. Contemporary American Poetry

Book design by Tonya Namura using Latin Modern

Cover photo by Brad Ayers

Author photo by Andy Ayers

Night Rain Press is an imprint of Night Rain Books

Night Rain
PO Box 445
Tillamook, OR 97141

Night.Rain.Press@gmail.com
http://NightRainPress.com

for my brother, Alan

Red Cross Volunteer
 who developed Leukemia
  eight years after being on the scene
   at the World Trade Center on 9/11

Acknowledgments

Sincere thanks to the literary journals *Escape Into Life, Floating Bridge Review, Naugatuck River Review, Snake Nation Review*, and to the anthologies *Bared* (Les Femmes Folles) and *Fire On Her Tongue* (Two Sylvias Press) in which some of the poems in this collection previously appeared. Also, several poems appeared in my collection *Dance From Inside My Bones* (Snake Nation Press, 2007).

Warm thanks to the members of our poetry critique group: Kelli Russell Agodon, Ronda Broatch, Annette Spaulding Convy, Jeannine Hall Gailey, Holly Hughes, Janet Norman Knox, Jenifer Browne Lawrence, and Natasha Kochicheril Moni.

Profound thanks to Tonya Namura, my amazing book designer.

Gracious thanks to my father-in-law Brad for creating a beautiful photograph for the cover.

Heartfelt thanks to my husband Andy for all his love and encouragement, plus taking dozens of author photos of me until we got the angle just right.

As always, deep gratitude to all my poetry mentors, especially, Ottone 'Ricky' Riccio who met me at the threshold of poetry and welcomed me in; Patricia Fargnoli who believed in me until I could too; Cecilia Woloch who said making poems is a gift and a responsibility; Joan Larkin who taught me to be fierce about my own truth; and last, but never least, my third grade teacher, Mrs. Pearl Sarfaty who kissed fuchsia lipstick wings on my cheeks and dubbed me a poet.

Poems of family are difficult, but necessary. My hope is that what shines through these are love, forgiveness, and redemption.

CONTENTS

1. Nursing Home

Woman Reading With Peaches	5
Bulimic Love	7
The Elusive Zen of Housework	9
The Honeymoon Photo, Niagara Falls 1955	11
My Mother's Favorite Expression	12
My Two Deaths	13
Saturday Evening, Mid 1960s	15
Far Away Home	16
Someone Said We Always Want What We Can't Have	17
Betrothal	18
The Red Jacket	20
While the Bathtub is Filling	22
I Never Thought to Lay Down with My Father	23
My Father's Last Words	24
The Toe	25
To Mother in Her Blindness	26
Gardening Is Design in the 4th Dimension	28
Bone Loss	30
Unspoken Early Elegy For My Mother	34
Exception to the Rule of Macular Degeneration	38
Why I Am a Writer	40
The Red Blood Man	43
A Question of Dementia	45
Beneath What's Known	46
When I Identify Your Body	48
In My Dreams I Draw Circles, But None of Their Edges Touch	50
The Path	52
Visitation	54

Stoop-Sitting With Daddy	56
The Rainy Day Is Today	58
Red Jacket Motel, Elmira, NY, 1968	62

2. THE DEAD BOY

The Dead Boy Is Diagnosed	67
The Dead Boy Sings In Heaven	69
The Dead Boy Teaches Me About Godzilla	71
The Dead Boy and the Storm	73
The Dead Boy As Artist	74
The Dead Boy Likes Ketchup	76
The Dead Boy and Barbie	77
The Dead Boy Likes Chocolate Best	79
The Dead Boy Tricks Me	81
Play Dead	83
The Dead Boy Babysits	85
The Dead Boy Goes Hungry	87
Rare Photo of the Dead Boy	88
The Dead Boy Relaxes	89
The Dead Boy Is Mugged	90
The Dead Boy Cruises	92
The Dead Boy Gets Engaged	94
The Dead Boy's Father Dies	96
The Dead Boy Becomes a Father	98
The Dead Boy Saves Lives	99
The Dead Boy Shrinks	100
The Dead Boy Enlists	101
The Dead Boy Inspires Me to Ice	103
A Mitzvah For the Dead Boy	105
A Mother's Day Gift For the Dead Boy	106
The Dead Boy's Last Words to Me	107
The Dead Boy Teaches Me About Impermanence	109

The Dead Boy's Eyes Radiate Light	112
The Dead Boy Visits the Hayden Planetarium	113
Godzilla and The Dead Boy's Doppelganger	115
ABOUT THE AUTHOR	119

The Dead Boy Sings In Heaven

1. Nursing Home

Woman Reading With Peaches
after the painting by Matisse

It is late June, the honeymoon
over for six months,
the bob you got
for your ceremony
grown to cover your ears.

Your fingers curl around
a plait, twirl it over and again.

The day bright and humid,
ink from the newspaper
stains your forearm.

You take a bite of a peach.
Even the sweet juice
leaves a bitter aftertaste.

Nothing tastes good any more.

You're wearing a loose mustard-
colored housecoat,
the only clothing you have
comfortable enough
to accommodate
the expanding belly
growing a being inside you.

Your husband is elated,
and both sides' parents.

When you close your eyes
you still see the life you wished for
like a movie clip on a Mobius reel—
wearing a smart, tailored Joan Crawford
suit and high heels,

leaving for a summer in the Hamptons
with your equally famous friends—
not the life your eyes open to.
Your house a too-tight box,
low ceilings, narrow windows,
a radio your only companion.

Your husband machines
battleship parts over in Brooklyn,
while you sit at the kitchen table,
light leaching away until
the entire room is shadow.

Your husband will find you like this,
unable to explain what you're doing,
so still, so silent.
Are you sick? he'll ask.

You will reassure him
the baby's fine,
then fry up some eggs for his supper
on a muggy evening
a few months before
your life irrevocably changes
and you become the word
you never wanted—

Mother.

Bulimic Love

Whenever I talked back
or got caught
eating cookies before supper,
mother sent me to my room
where all the books I loved
provided multiple escape routes.

Had she known locking me up
with words was like sending me off
in a rowboat on the high seas,
maybe she would have
sent me to the basement instead.

I was gone for hours inside
the worlds of books
and inside the tales in my head,
where planets existed
no one knew about but me,
like *Blotetopia*, where fat girls
were princesses praised for
the size of their stomachs.

If only I could have lived on a diet
of language, I would have become
thin and wise,
but always a time would come
when my belly would rumble
and I'd open my door
and grumble into the hall,
I'm starving in here!

And like the bad mother she was
to this very naughty little girl,
Mother would usher me
down the hall to the small kitchen

that was more like a library
of forbidden foods.

She'd unlock
the paltry pantry of her heart,
let me eat and eat and eat,
but it was all
empty calories.

The Elusive Zen of Housework

My mother's eyes red from Comet fumes,
a cigarette glowed
from the corner of her mouth.

Dad's armpit-stained, wadded-up
t-shirt soaked in a puddle
by her bare feet.

From the portable radio,
crooner Al Martino pledged his heart.

My mother crouched to scrub
inside the refrigerator,
its former contents overflowing
the trash can.

What are you doing? I asked.

Taking advantage of the blackout,
she answered, her cigarette bobbing,
ash dropping to the yellow linoleum.

I pointed to an ice cream carton
leaking a pool of mint chip.
Can I have some? I said.

Go ahead, she answered.

I sat cross-legged on the floor,
scooping green goo with my fingers,
sucking each sticky digit clean.

Mother and I stayed like that
for a long while.

Life felt good to me.

The lesson of the moment—
that any bad circumstance
could be transformed into a feast,
or an opportunity to make things shine.

A seven-year-old,
I did not think to question
how she could stand
all that housework,
the awful fumes,

or ask what went on in her head,
as perspiration poured off her brow,
her back bent into the rhythmic scouring.

All the while, the radio broadcast
idyllic love songs.

My mother did not sing,
did not even
hum along.

The Honeymoon Photo, Niagara Falls 1955,

on the dresser in my parents' bedroom
set in a mirrored frame
dusted once a week
for twenty-five years—
a black and white of a couple
seated in a restaurant booth,
his arm around her,
her hand patting her short hairdo,
his gap-toothed grin,
her eyes squinting,
smushed remains of cake
on both their plates,
two coffee cups,
hers lipstick-kissed,
his brimming over into the saucer—
suddenly,
inexplicably
disappears.

When I ask
where the photo went,
my mother says,
I have no idea
what picture
you could mean.
My father,
misty-eyed, sighs, says,
Sometimes things aren't
how they seem.

My Mother's Favorite Expression

Not *I love you,*
not *Let me help,*
not *Do you want something to eat,*
not *Do your homework,*
not *No elbows on the table,*
not *Go to your room,*
not *Shut up,*
not even *Stop bugging me,*
but *Enough already,*
Enough already,
Enough!

My Two Deaths

1.
My next door neighbor,
Aunt Mickey, tells me
about the time the firemen
came to my house.

Mother had blown out
the pilot light in the oven,
then turned up the gas
and lit a match.

The explosion knocked
Aunt Mickey off her feet
in her own kitchen,
where she was cooking sauce.

Aunt Mickey says my mother
told the firemen
she was home alone.

But the firemen found
infant me amid the smoke,
lying on a charred blanket
under the kitchen table.

They almost thought me a doll
because I wasn't breathing.

2.
I'm choking
on a hard sour ball sucking candy
and floating up out of my body
as my mother laughs and laughs.

I am glad to fly far from her,
toward the light.

But a strange man rushes
through the screen door into
our dark room at the Catskills motel.

He grabs me by my legs,
shakes me upside down
until the candy comes free,
pops out of me.

I plummet headlong
back into my body,
coughing.

Dirty bastard,
Mother says.
She tears at the man's
shirt collar.
How dare you?
I was almost free
of the little bitch.

Saturday Evening, Mid 1960s

My father waters the small, square
lawn in front of our brick-faced,
ranch home with asbestos-
shingled siding.

Daddy holds his thumb over
the garden hose nozzle a certain way
so that the steady stream is magically
transformed to a fine spray.

I am watching from the screen door,
my fingers troubling a tiny defect
in the weave, working it into a full-fledged
hole insects will infiltrate.

I have a summer cold, so Mother has
forbidden me from going outside even though
it's so mild my father wears only his white
sleeveless undershirt & cotton plaid shorts.

There's a pale rainbow in the hose mist.
I want to call out to Daddy so he
can see it too, but I know he wouldn't hear me
over the rush of the liquid,

over the cars thumping by in the street,
over the song he's surely humming.
My father won't be able to hear me
for years, and by then, it will be too late.

Far Away Home

Our car plowed through darkness
on the deserted Belt Parkway,
pushing the island of Manhattan back.
Mother and Daddy didn't speak to one another,
her puffing away at cigarettes,
the red glow at their tips
sparking to life with each drawn breath,
the exhalations sighing out smoke.

My older brother, my torturer,
on the seat next to me, was finally snoring.
I leaned back and looked out the window
at the stars and the brilliant lit-up top
of the Empire State building.
I knew it was really a spaceship
keeping tabs on me until the day
my mission observing earthlings was over.

All done, I'd climb aboard triumphant,
return to my true planet,
the one where parents stay in love forever
and there are no older brothers.
From my command seat in the capsule,
I'd be able to watch the earth shrink
to a teeny tiny blue marble,
reach out, put it in my pocket.

Someone Said We Always Want What We Can't Have

It seems not a thing in the universe is moving.
The leaves on all the trees
are completely still,
No airplanes are flying overhead.

Even our little earth isn't spinning.
Our littler moon isn't circling,
that right now is lit white,
looking tiny and cold

as a snowball I once hurled
at my older brother,
only to be pummeled later
with ice chunks and his fists.

I looked up at the sky
while I took my beating,
wanting only to be a cloud
passing over the moon's happy squint.

Tonight, I want to be that little girl again
the day before life got hard.
If I could have, I would have learned how
to dance from inside my bones.

Imagine me now,
twirling and twirling and twirling,
propeller-like in the ghostly moonlight
and not a thing to stop me.

Betrothal

My father is driving my boyfriend
home to Astoria,
the diagonally opposite side of Queens
from where we live,
a foreign country to me
who's never ventured further
than two bus routes
in my twenty years.

Still his trusted little girl then, though
I am not a virgin many times over,
have even done the deed in the back seat
of Daddy's Pontiac parked in the driveway,
while he snored in front of a Knicks game.

It's January, a sudden drop in temperature,
and a light drizzle transforms
Queens Boulevard to skating rink—
cars colliding all around us.

Safe driver, no accident in forty years,
my father steers into the skid
as ice tricks our tires.

We spin—
the world horizontal stripes
before we hit.

Lucky, only a slight bump.

The other driver, a twenty-something man,
springs like a tiger from his Toyota,
growling threats,
I'll take your house,
I'll take every valuable you have.

A policeman appears,
jots plate numbers.

I keep saying, *Oh no,
oh no, oh no,*
staring at Daddy,
confounded by his composure
at being blamed
for an act of god.

My father, next to the officer,
seems smaller, and new wrinkles
surround the wrinkles
around his eyes.

I will marry that boyfriend
not long after,
who there holds me in his arms
in the frigid wreck of one evening
'til I quiet down,

wishing then, as now,
Daddy to be the one
patting my hair
and whispering,
*Shush baby,
shush.*

The Red Jacket
after a painting by Matisse

I never wanted you, my mother says.

I have heard this before,
sometimes screamed at high decibel,
sometimes stated matter-of-factly,
like now, across telephone distance.

I imagine my mother's wearing
the red velvet housecoat
trimmed in gold brocade
with generous pockets
that hold her four packs
of menthols a day.
Her smoking jacket,
I always joked.

It's after ten pm so
her hair's probably wrapped
in toilet paper, tucked under
her pink flowered sleeping cap,
though she's hours away
from her usual bedtime.

I have called to tell her
my husband tried to kill me,
tonight, after his fourth
glass of whiskey,
after I said maybe
he should slow down.

I don't know anyone
in this new town but him.
I don't have a job yet,
or a bank account.

We've been married ten days
after dating long distance
for ten months.

I have a college degree,
and no idea how this can be
happening to me.

My husband is a businessman
and white collar men aren't
supposed to be violent, just boring.

He tried to strangle me,
I tell my mother.
I was choking,
then everything went dark.
When I woke up it was just me
alone in the apartment.

You should have let him
kill you, my mother says.
It's your fault for making
him mad. Can't do anything
right, not even be a good wife.
You know I never wanted you,
it was your father who
insisted on a second child.

Mom, I need help, I say
What am I going to do?

That's your problem you
cry-baby, my mother says.
Don't call home again unless
you're dead, she says
and slams the phone.

While the Bathtub is Filling

The mirror reports that I am starting to
resemble my mother, the way she looked

that time I went into her bedroom without knocking,
saw her breasts—two weighted-down plastic bags,

bloated, slow-swinging pendulums.
I decided right then to die at eighteen,

in the prime of perkiness and elasticity.
Last year, my mother showed me a fat scar

where her left breast used to be.
It looked as if a red snake slithered

out of her heart and hid his head
in the brush of her armpit.

The longer I stared, the more I recognized the
creature above her belly for what it was—life.

Nothing about nakedness was ever that lovely.
My mother's survived this halving,

that scar, a red brooch of honor
making me proud to be a woman like her.

In a moment, when the tub is finally full,
I'll forget the mirror, all these musings,

lie back in the pale green bath,
and feel the warm water work its magic,

making buoyant, bobbing apples
of my two old gals.

I Never Thought to Lay Down with My Father

but that July afternoon I held him as I would a lover,
his body half the weight it had been, all cancer.
The sun beamed dust dancers through the transom.
A fan fussed back and forth billowing damp air.
I touched the prickly place above my father's ear,
bristle-shadow pretending hair might grow some more.

In my mother's place on the bed, face to face,
with daddy sobbing, *I'm not ready to go...*
so much I want to accomplish.
The bedspread's embroidered roses, forged levity.
Where once was sweat & muscle, dry folds, emptied flesh
Everywhere he was fragile, my fingers kissed.
An old rolodex clock clicked squares of numerals.

I held nothing back but words and tears,
none and countless.

My Father's Last Words

All bone and unwarmable feet,
alone with the crash cart team,
my father died.

Thrashing with unbelievable force,
combatting it the whole way,
the attending nurse reported.
He didn't say anything though.

What we will always remember
from the muddled day before,
eight of us huddled by his bed,
visiting rules ignored for someone
this close to the end, and Daddy said,

Anyone bring a bat and glove,
we've got enough for a team?

The Toe

Despite how mystically moonlight snakes a path across the lake tonight, and because love is the property solely of country music, and since Plath's bell jar of pain runneth over for all eternity, I will write only of a toe—a plain enough thing—the fourth toe on my mother's right foot and how each day, despite my bathing it, my application of greasy salve, the wrapping and rewrapping to apply just enough pressure, it continued to blacken, the toe like a banana past sweetness to the other side of neglect, or salt beef dried to jerky, tenderness abandoned to gristle, so I write this about my mother's toe, how the doctor tells us it must go as if speaking of an ingrown hair or a splinter, as if it were nothing important, nothing a person spent her whole life walking on, on grass, over damp-mopped kitchen linoleum, dancing backwards on in high heels over slick-waxed ballrooms floors, or in babyhood grabbed for all googly-eyed and occasionally even sucked, this dried up toe that oddly causes mother no pain, and yet when the doctor says the toe must go, this woman who was a marble column at father's bedside during his failed chemo, who later presided over father's grave, stolid as a granite headstone, and not long after, this woman who sat composed as Rodin's "Bather" as another doctor spoke the word mastectomy to her, and all through radiation wore a Mona Lisa smile, this woman does a thing I'd never seen her do, my mother cries, sobs, weeps, exhausts all the tissues in the doctor's stainless dispenser, and keeps crying over this very small rotten toe, this calamity of losing what one least expected to lose.

To Mother in Her Blindness

Alone in your house,
the dust you can no longer see
due to macular degeneration
piles up like all your disappointments,
the curtains stained with nicotine tar.

Shrunken six inches of height,
you hobble with your cane,
to meet me at the door.

A tenderness should fill me.

This house was never my home
and the sad grime is pitiful, nothing more.
Truly, there was never a house
you made me feel at home.

Even in the country of your womb,
you rejected me early.
Neighbors claimed my crib-bound cries
went on for hours.
Bottle-fed, I grew up hungry, fat.

Self-hatred may be a gene
you passed on to me
through your absence,
Love a word your lips
couldn't form.
Instead, you dubbed me your
fat-ugly-pig child.

Now, you tell me about
your friends' children,
how well they treat their mothers.

I could retort,
What you sow, you reap,
but keep silent instead,
feeling guilty.

I was always there,
waiting within
the short reach of your arms
and wanted little more
than your softness around me,
your ashy smell.

You are an old woman, burdened,
and if you were not my mother,
I would swell with pity,
instead of loving you
tenaciously,
beyond all reason,
as I always have,
in my own blindness.

Gardening Is Design in the 4th Dimension
A rambling elegy on the anniversary of Daddy's death

More for myself, for the missing breath, the space it leaves, the listening you were, the talking I was, all the words filling up with no place to go now. I miss the non-ruffling of feathers, the sponge absorption.

Blame is what I call mourning. Human. The sky has no language for this. It paints and unpaints itself all day, rearranges its hair, spruces with a few well-placed sailboats. I would like you to take me back, but how does one ask for the ears of the dead?

I exhale shadows. Sunlight kisses the sparrows that chatter all morning. Nights, fish discuss theories of harmonics, while those birds dream of places so deep inside the earth, sound is coal, iron, beryl.

Where does it come from, this need for talk? My words wing at you like moths. Will you cook them omelets for breakfast on Sundays, teach them how to play pinochle? Your heart turns a deaf ear. The ground breathes a sigh.

Daddy, I do not miss you only in the rain. Also on days where the sun is imperative. Squirrels make fools of themselves along the fence. Humor is another shade of disgrace. I love you—grit in the tincture.

My stomach growls its bared teeth. Memory asks how high? Regret says, *leave a message, no one is available.* Tears like cloudburst. These are homeless times for my lips.

The back of my throat misses you like a diver, the sunken ship. Fly up through depths, thoughts, bless someone, somewhere. Bless hands that lift this page, lay down a phone without anyone to call. Bless even the phone, its silence the tongue in God's mouth.

BONE LOSS

i.
Bone loss has shrunken my mother's height, so I am eye-view with the top of her head. Once Lucille-Ball-red, mother's hair now hoary, sparse. Hair that is mostly scalp, baby-talc white. Should I rock her, sing her a lullaby?

Time's mineral deposits dull mother's eyes as if with calcite, lime. She is legally blind, but sees well enough to scrutinize my wrinkles, reckon me past prime. Mine is a worried face, older than hers if one tallies by tears spent, salt shed. Lot's wife turned to salt for sorrow's sake, turned against the will of God. I will not turn from Mother's gaze.

This is a house of cave dwellers. The small flicker of television, cold camp fire. Cigarette smoke heats Mother's lips. I lift the tepid ceramic curve of a coffee mug to my lips, like kissing bone. Outside it's summer. Inside this house of murk, we are without season.

ii.
In nicotine kitchen light I read Primo Levi. The words are flakes of ash across pages. In Auschwitz, the body's story became one charred word, clumped with chunks of bone, unsayable. Here, death is not translated into speech. Mother coughs, spits, lights another cigarette. She measures her hours with broadcast news, cornucopic medications, the size, consistency, and number of bowel movements, hers, mine. Like a Nazi, I command her with the silent German tongue of my heart, die faster—*tot bald sien*. Like a Jew, she refuses.

iii.
Mother's installed herself in my father's easy chair, still called *his* chair, though he's thirteen years beneath the earth. Her bunioned, elevated feet bulked with several pairs of socks appear almost *challah*-like, the loaves of the holy day. We do not bake bread, mother and I. We do not light *Shabbos* candles. We do not say our blessings, mother and I. God left us the day my father died, taking piety with him. His was a grizzled, lung cancer death that guzzled the fluidity of his thoughts as well as his flesh, picked him skeletal, contorted him in shit-stained hospital sheets. Could anyone love God after that? Mother went on smoking four packs a day, even as my father lay dying. Outside Columbia University Hospital, she sent smoke signals up to the no-one in heaven who would not read them, smoke signals up to the no-one in heaven who would not respond. She's reclining in his chair now, watching the weekend weather forecast, burning Salem after Salem, smoke stopped at the ceiling, a cypher of yellow stain painting itself there, pentagraphic, incomprehensible. Leisure is not so easy (even in my father's chair).

iv.
Though I offer to help her to the toilet, adult diapers bestow mother the choice to boil in her own acid. She's bold in her obstinacy, announcing every pee with the savage glee of a three year old. I don't actually want to clean her, meanness, or revenge for the diapers I pickled in until infection bulged my bladder, sour sores prickled my infant ass. Later on, a neighbor lady came by daily to change me, telling everyone she could smell the pus from

across the street. Yet, each day mother denies me the chore when I try, refusing to let me to touch her, shouting, *You're killing me, you're killing me,* if I get too close. Occasionally, the urine stink overwhelms and I attempt to wrestle her will. She bites, draws blood.

Every other day, the nurse's aide arrives, a dark-skinned angel, Mother calls *the schvartzer* behind her back. After a childhood of crossed arms I yearned to be held in, fisted hands I yearned to have hold mine, I marvel at this intimacy Mother allows, how she opens so completely to a stranger. I yearn for Mother's cheek bone against my own.

v.
This was not what I intended to write, something ugly about the living mother, about the daughter. I meant to wait, to resurrect her better after death, to figure back that woman of so many years ago, the one I never knew, grinning from Mardi Gras Polaroids, a gleam in her cat-eyed gaze. I meant to invent ways to barhop with her, sip Martinis and flip our hair at service boys. I meant to revive that shy little girl from the crumbling black and whites cornered into Grandma's album, she huddled in lace and curls, face always tipped down, clutching her own mother's hand. It would have been something to give that child a doll dressed in purple velvet, a stuffed bear with real glass eyes, watch a smile pump its way across her plump cheeks. Sinful sexpot, innocent cherub, I could write my way into her heart if only she were not here now, not my living, reeking, screeching Mother.

vi.

Mother will never tell me about the old days, nothing about her childhood, the games she played, the songs she sang along with the radio, the boys who borrowed then broke her heart. I'll never know what made her loathe the life she married herself into, despise the children she bore and bottle fed. My father was a mostly mild pious man who adored his wife as if she walked on water.

Deep in the bones, we are Jews, mother, daughter, sisters of Eve. Jews not by prayer, but by story—the story of Diaspora, dispersion, dissolution. In this tale there is but one testament and no resurrection, no blood of the messiah, no body of the host to spare us our original sin. On our tongues we taste iron, then close our eyes, certain we deserve the dirt shoveled over us, even as we are still breathing.

Unspoken Early Elegy For My Mother
    after Richard Blanco

I arrive at the nursing home with a box
of sugarless chocolates and a handful of
enlarged family photos of our old brick-front
ranch house in Queens.

In one photo, Mother's hair is swept up
in a bouffant do at my brother's Bar Mitzvah.
In another photo taken at my college graduation,
my arm around her, Mother puffs away
at a cigarette, stares off into the distance.

I lean over Mother's wheelchair
to kiss her hello,
and she says, *Thank god.*
I thought you were lost.
You were supposed to be here already.

No, I tell her, *actually I'm a day early.*

Already, you're lying, she says. *Stop it.*

For my mother I can never be right or true.

I guide her to the library where a muted TV
is tuned to soap operas no one watches.
I sit opposite her at the wooden table,
observe that her floral, flannel housecoat
much like the ones she wore even when young,
bears a brown stain over the place
her left breast used to be,
a stain in her near-blindness
I am certain she cannot see.

We have so little to talk about.
She does not care to hear my poems,
since they are not poems to her
if they don't rhyme.

I was seven years old
the first time I showed
Mother a poem—
fall, leaves blown off tree limbs
like soldiers dying.
Mother crumpled the paper
into a ball, tossed it to the floor,
hollered, *Pick up your trash.*

And she doesn't want news
of my four cats because
cats are nothing more than
big rats according to her.
*Why don't you drown them
in the bathtub,* Mother says
if I ever I mention them.

So I hold out the photos I've brought,
at an angle,
better for macular degenerated eyes,
remind her of parts of the past she enjoys.

The house looks smaller than I remember,
she says. *That's not my hair, there must
have been a raccoon on my head.
You finished college? That's news to me.*

Not wanting to argue, I ask if she's going
to activities. *I go to the music,* she says,
that's really the only good thing here.
And you'd be happy to know I wrote a poem.

Can you recite it? I say.
She says, *Mary had a little lamb,*
its fur was black as night.
When Mary went to shear the wool,
the lamb gave quite a fight.
It's better than anything you write,
she says, and I agree.

Over sugar-free chocolates we talk
about the weather and other
inconsequential things.
She doesn't want to speak
about people who have died
or living folks who
never come to see her.

Mother just wants us to sit,
pretend we're at the family home
back in Queens,
where at any moment,
she'll rise up from stroke-atrophied legs,
stroll into her tiny kitchen
with its laminate cabinets and countertops,
its outdated brown appliances,
to cook us up a hot meal
like she used to nearly every night
the first eighteen years of my life.

Even though her pet names for me
have always been
fatso and *fat ugly pig*,
all this mother wants to do
is just feed her *fatso* child
one last time.

Exception to the Rule of Macular Degeneration

My mother, legally blind,
stares past me
at the television that is turned off.

On the bedside table behind her
the Yankees pregame show
murmurs from the radio.

I have been failing to find a subject
my mother wants to talk about,
things she once loved impossible now.

Stop playing with your hair,
my mother scolds.

I realize I have been pulling
my fingers through my coarse curls,
an ugly, nervous habit.

You can see that? I say.

Of course, my mother says.

I fold my hands in my lap.
For this moment I am my mother's
unruly little girl again.

You know, my mother says,
you don't look your age.

I am not her little girl any longer.
I am my mother's middle-aged daughter.

Whose age do I look? I say.

Very funny, my mother says.

Neither of us laugh.

Why I Am a Writer

I show Mother a blown-up photo
of our old dog Apache,
two decades dead,
and my father,
one decade dead,
both of them
seated at the dining room table
in chairs,
both smiling.

Apache wasn't really
allowed to sit at the table
like a person,
but since it was Passover
and he jumped into
Elijah's empty chair,
we let it go.

My mother smiles, points
a shaky finger at our dog.
Oh that's Apache, she says.
My good doggy.

Who else is in the photo?

No one, she says, squinting.

I insist, tapping my index
finger over Daddy's
yarmulked head.
Who's that?

Who is that? she says.

*That's your husband
of thirty-five years,* I say.
Daddy.

No, you're lying,
she says, *that's not
my husband.
That's not your father either.
I never had any husband.*

Then who was my father?

*The red blood man
was your father.
That's a picture of some
bum who came to the house
and ate all my food
and never gave me a dime.*

My father worked
as a machinist,
then a maintenance man
to support us.
Daddy paid for everything,
I say, *so you could stay home
with my brother and me.*

No, she says.
raising her thin brows
and her voice.
*I had six children
and supported them all
myself by selling pencils.*

I nod, not wanting
to agitate her further.

Maybe she's remembering
a movie plot or something
she dreamt, or maybe
that's the story of her life
she means for me to write.

The Red Blood Man

*I'm scared
the red blood man
will get you too,*
my mother says.

Her skin is translucent
with blue veins,
her face shrunken
into her shoulders.
She's staring down
at her hands
nested in her lap.

Someone's dressed
Mother in the new floral
nightgown I brought
and the new navy blue sweater.
She smells clean today,
like talcum powder.

*Where did you see this
Red Blood Man?* I say.

He comes in my room at night,
she says, *and paces the aisle
between the two beds.*

What does he look like? I say.

I can't tell, she says.
He's tall, I think.

When she's lying in bed,
everyone's tall.

*He murdered your
brother,* she continues.
*He took your brother's
blood in a needle,
then injected him with
leukemia.*

*That not how he contracted
leukemia,* I say.

He did, my mother says.
Her hands grip the arms
of her wheelchair.
She lifts her head, looks past me
to the muted TV across the room
where a game show's playing.

I'm immune, she says.
He can't kill me.

I am your daughter, I say,
maybe I'm immune too.

My mother turns from
the TV, looks me in the face.
Her grip on the wheelchair
loosens and she nods.
Maybe you are, she says.

A Question of Dementia

Do you remember when
I showed you the picture
of a cat I painted using

lime green magic marker
and hot pink nail polish
that soaked through the paper

and stained both our hands?

My mother regards
her liver spotted skin,
wiggles her fingers.

No, she says.

No, I say.
Neither do I.

Beneath What's Known

My mother saw ants on the floor
where there were none,
macular degeneration
making so much
less clear,
imagination often filling in
for the blurs.

Such that, there in the room
at the care center
an industrious tribe of insects
took over the invisible blanket
at our feet, a ruined picnic.

I wondered whether tuna
or egg salad, and whether
I should attempt rescue.
*What would you like
me to do?* I asked her.

Just look at them, she said,
*Just look.
It's like they've never seen
food before,* she said.
Never eaten.

And where I supposed
her face would show
consternation, was none.
Instead, her tongue curled
over her lower lip, childlike.

So, I looked and I looked
until I saw those same ants too,
their brown-beaded segments

tripping over one another to take
infinitesimal bites of an apple.

Not a particularly large apple,
either, just a medium Macintosh,
but for them, a feast without end.

And for my mother,
from a life so curtailed
by age and regret,
a few moments of pleasant
distraction.

In the end, even a ravaged
picnic can be joy.

When I Identify Your Body

The funeral director
leads me to the dim room
with striped-pink wallpaper.
The only furniture is the table
on which your body is laid,
draped in a shroud,
as is the Jewish tradition.

Your face is unwrapped,
your eyes are closed,
but your mouth is open—
perpetually open—
as it was in life,
even when you
weren't speaking.

For these last years,
after the many strokes
having given up smoking,
your mouth formed
a permanent,
unanswerable question—
What to do now?

How alive you look
with your eyes closed,
as if only dozing.

When I touch your cheek,
your skin feels so smooth
and warm, that I wonder
if this is your idea of a joke,
if at any moment the hoax
of your death will be undone.

You'll open your eyes
and say, *Not so fast.*
You're not getting rid
of me that easy.

The truth, Mother, is
I'll never be free of you,
because you are part of me
like storm cloud to rain.

Maybe it wasn't your job
to love me in this life,
but rather my role
to teach you what love is
supposed to be,
how it holds fast
even in the darkest hours,
for hours and hours,
a lifespan.

If this was my mission,
Mother, I have failed you—
miserably.

All I can do now is
ring the silent bell,
summon the funeral director
to let it be known
the body they have laid out
is indeed the body
of my beloved.

In My Dreams I Draw Circles, But None of Their Edges Touch
after a painting by Fereidun Shokatfard

I wait for word from you.

Is your new place free
from crooked trees?

Free from those who steal
your blood,
prick by prick?

Are you eating almonds
glazed with honey,
your resurrected
teeth sharp and sturdy?

I have heard of yellow
skies, of wind
becoming ravens.

And do you walk again,
Mother, where you are,
legs strong as stones,
steps light as smoke?

I imagine you singing
Andrews Sisters' hits
as if they were your own,
refusing autographs.

Our long ago dog with golden fur
crouches by your heels.

Your newly-healed son brings
you useful trinkets,
coffee mugs and ashtrays.

What news do you want of me?

Since you died,
my books have become deserts,
regret swarms my throat
like hornets.

I speak now only in whispers,
each syllable a damp match.

THE PATH
But I, being poor, have only my dreams;
I have spread my dreams under your feet;
Tread softly because you tread on my dreams.
               —William Butler Yeats

Sometimes moonlight piles up
the way snowdrifts did back when
I was a kid—shoulder height or more,
and Daddy would pull on his poor, thin
galoshes, go out
to shovel us a path
from the side door to where his car
ballooned in its tomb of snow.

My father was a lone engine,
puffing steam,
shoveling, shoveling, shoveling,
then seeding salt-melt
as if feeding a yard full of chickens.
None of us ever thought to go out
to help or keep him company in the cold.

In my obsession with finger-painting
bold flowers and cat faces in the vapor
on storm door glass, I forgot to ask
when Daddy came back in, flushed,
whistling and stamping his feet
to rid them of slush,
if he was ever lonely
in that hushed world out there.

Tonight, waist-deep in moonlight,
I comprehend no matter how much snow
we clear, how much salt we sow,
though dear ones may lend a hand,

ultimately, it's the path inside us
we're alone on—this life, a sole pursuit
to keep our footing sure.

VISITATION

Today is an unusual day, here
where the sky slips into the
burnished pewter light
that precedes a snowfall,
here where the temperatures
rarely dip below freezing.

Here, where I have moved
to escape the east coast
blizzards of my childhood,
snowdrifts often taller than I was,
always small for my age.

I wait at the window
for the flurry,
for some movement
in a landscape that is
still as expectation.

I step outside under fir boughs
still unshaken, under cedars
silent as the birds that are
somewhere else,
air tasting metallic
on my tongue.

Like a soft humming,
it begins all at once—
a veil of flakes—
the white of the sky,
the white of the snow,
my shoulders coat with white,
eyelashes mascara in white,
my whole body baptized white.

I lean back, open my face
to the soft storm.

Shortly, I can no longer tell
what direction the snow is going,
and I am lifted skyward—
lifted in time,
lifted back to you mother
damp and warm
from your shower,
your body enveloped
in talc, sweet smelling silk
evident on your skin everywhere.

When I run to embrace you,
a white powder cloud rises up
between us, suspends there
floating over us, Mother,
around us, unstoppable
even now that your pale skin
rests in dark, dark clouds of earth.

Stoop-Sitting With Daddy

> *Qué hambre*
> *de saber*
> *cuántas*
> *estrellas tiene el cielo!*
>   —Pablo Neruda

Late one moonless night,
I sneak onto the brick front stoop
of the house where I grew up
and sit, pulling my knees
close to my chest to muffle
the clamor of my clanging heart.

The new owners have not tended
the home, nor the yew bushes
Daddy clipped into goblet shapes,
hours of back-straining labor.
The grass is mostly crab now,
with a battalion of dandelions
that never infiltrated
on my father's watch.

It's late August, a cricket-less
calm settled over the sticky,
mosquito-studded air,
and the sky overhead full
of constellations.

I am reminded of those endless
summer nights,
when doused in bug spray,
Daddy and I used to count
the stars out loud,
a father-daughter song
with no lyrics but numbers.

Daddy was Orion, the bull-slayer,
brave hero, and I was
his little bear,
ready to slake his thirst
by running inside
to put on the kettle,
pour a cup of Sanka,
hot, black.

And my tongue almost tastes
our favorite ice cream,
Breyers' mint chip,
always only one
aqua Melamine dish
for our two-spoon,
stoop-sitting happiness.

Daddy pointed out constellations too,
until my eyes blurred from squinting
to make the patterns match their names,
until my sleepy-headedness
made the sky seem filled with nothing
but bright, luminous sheep.

Right now, a shooting star
ghosts across the sky,
and in my mind,
the screen door squeaks open—
Daddy arriving to sit beside me
on the stoop and count,
one last time.

The Rainy Day Is Today

Three weeks early for Mother's Day,
three years after my mother's death
from a stroke in her sleep,
preceded by five years of her dementia,
I discover inside a box of Curad bandages
(small round-shaped, quilted discs)
a bank envelope with Mother's handwriting—
a simple, clean cursive *Lana*.

The bandages are for sensitive skin,
breathable fabric, and ouchless.
My mother always said
I had thin skin.

A secret you don't know
is that I am a hoarder.
When I find a consumable product
that does well what is necessary,
I buy enough to hold me for a year.
Though all too often I lose interest
and the goods collect dust
in overstuffed cupboards.

Those Curad bandages are two decades
old, bought as a close-out lot
of a dozen boxes so I could daily
cover a diminutive cyst on my left arm
that grew back the week after
the dermatologist excised it.
A dot of latex to prevent
the sun's harmful rays.

I stopped using the protection
after my father died of lung cancer,

him being my last living relative
who actually loved me.

Without him, our nuclear family
of my mother, my brother, and I
became a spokeless, radioactive wheel.

To say that the mother-daughter
relationship was gamma decay
would be gross understatement.

In her decade-long decline
toward death, Mother
never reached stability or reason,
no hugs or *I love yous*,
no regrets except birthing me.

So when and why and how did
she place the envelope in a box
of bandages that have relocated
with me half a dozen times,
and from east to west coast?

And did I mention, the envelope
bearing the insignia of a defunct
bank, contains five crisp
twenty dollar bills, 1999 series,
Jackson with the big head,
(not the colorful version
that came later)?

My mother tucked away
one hundred dollars for me.
I guess for a rainy day.

What if I never saw the envelope
and tossed the money?
I would never have known
about the sweetest thing
she's ever done for me.

And on this record-breaking hot
Seattle morning, when I decide
once more to cover my cyst
against further damage,
I come upon this gift—
unexpected, generous, and strange.

Perhaps it's a form of apology
or admission of guilt,
however inadequate and late.

Somehow in her head
did she calculate
the sum total reparation
for calling me unspeakable names
and wishing me dead
uncountable times—
five glaring Jacksons,
one hundred smackers?

Can any amount compensate
for the absence of Mothering?

And yet, I am inclined to be
delighted by this sudden windfall
from a ghost who I can hear
saying, very clearly,

*Don't spend it all in one place,
you stupid bitch.*

Red Jacket motel, Elmira, NY, 1968
after Richard Blanco

I thought I forgot everything...

The Red Jacket Motel off Route 17
just outside of Elmira in Lowman,
New York, should still be boasting
of its lodge-like wood-paneled rooms.
My brother and I should still be
fighting over who gets the bed
closest to the AC unit since
summer in the Southern Tier
of New York state is a muggy,
mosquito-infested affair.
After the seemingly never-ending
car trip from the city with
all the windows rolled down
my mother, father, brother and I
are all drenched in sweat
as if we bathed in a swamp
because we were too poor
to afford a used car equipped
with air conditioning.

I thought I forgot everything...

My father should still be hovering
over the AC unit in the motel room,
his damp driving clothes shed
strewn on the bed, the steel-wool
curly hair on his bare chest blowing
in the chill air, him luxuriating,
waiting for the rest us to change
into our swimming clothes
so we can take a dip in
The Red Jacket's onsite pool

that I will nearly drown in
when my brother holds my head
down and I struggle until
I see my dead grandfather
reaching out his big arms toward me.

I thought I forgot everything...

My mother should still be
complaining about the food
at the pancake house,
how the eggs are too runny
and the steak too well done,
even though for the rest of us
dining out is exotic and delicious.
She's irked because we can't
afford a fancier restaurant even
on our extended weekend vacation.
My father, who wants to make
everyone happy, should still be
asking the white-haired waitress
to kindly allow his wife to send back
her plate for another dinner choice,
his blue eyes the sky at its most serene.

I thought I forgot everything...

My brother should still be twelve,
tying me to the motel room wing chair
with his bathrobe belt while our parents
are at a nearby bar ordering Manhattans,
having trusted him to be responsible enough
to care for his six-year old sister—he wasn't.
Now, I am forty-eight, driving the Southern Tier

looking for the Red Jacket Motel, for what
seemed to me back then like hell, but wasn't.
I want to blame my brother for never
letting me get close enough to love him
for the man—husband and father—
he grew into. So I try to find the motel
as if it will still be standing just as it was,
not the storage lot that's there instead.

I want to go back to the Red Jacket motel
with my family—mother, father, brother—
all gone, me an orphan on this earth now
(and even if we weren't poor
no amount of money
could have saved any of them),
go back to that chlorine-filled pool
and swim for my life, swim in
the gleaming, sunblessed liquid
as if the ripples remember them,
resuscitate them, as if in water
everyone you once loved
can be reclaimed.

2. The Dead Boy

The Dead Boy Is Diagnosed

For nearly eight years after
the twin towers fell, after
he rescued survivor after
survivor, my brother was fine.

Now, he can't lift his head.

The doctors say,
*Rare form of leukemia
from burning jet fuel,
smoke inhalation.*

The doctors say,
Things we can do to prolong life.

The doctors say,
Percentages.

They do not say,
Cure.

I say, *Yes,*
to being a bone marrow donor,
spit into the container
for minutes,
wait weeks for the results.

My DNA says, *No,
not a match.*

The dead boy and I
have so much in common—
bad mother,
bad luck,

bad teeth,
but not our marrow.

The doctors will not save my brother.
Neither can I.

All my memories shift,
become lies.

It is as if he never was
wholly alive,
once I know
how young
he's going to die.

This is how
my brother
becomes
the dead boy.

The Dead Boy Sings In Heaven

or at least I like to imagine he does.

The dead boy, my brother,
never sings at home.
We are not a musical family.

In our childhood house there is
cigarette ash on all the floors
and four black and white televisions,
one, at least,
always on the fritz.

There is sitcom canned-
laughter to go with
canned green beans for supper.

There is a mother whose eyes scald,
whose words tattoo scars
inside our skulls.

There is Daddy's *New York Post*
page turning silence.

So my older brother never sings.

Me, I scream in the basement
where no one can hear.
It's almost like song.

My brother plugs up his ears,
never owns a stereo,
never learns to whistle,
though Ed Sullivan lets in The Beatles.

God, even though I don't believe in you,
please put a song in the dead boy's
dead heart.

One song,
and I promise
I'll sing too.

The Dead Boy Teaches Me About Godzilla

1.

Is the monster a boy or girl? I say.
I press my face to the television screen
to see if I can tell.

Shut up! my brother says.

So you don't know either, I say.

A soda can smacks the back of my head.

The dead boy has dead-keen aim.

2.

Sometimes Godzilla resembles
an ordinary boy in a rubber suit
throwing a tantrum.

Other times Godzilla's a tiny toy
in a broken toy city.

Godzilla crushes apartment complexes,
flings cars, flips buses.

Godzilla screeches flames.
People run and scream.

Why is the monster so angry?
I ask the dead boy.

*Because his stupid sister
won't shut up!* my brother says.

I think the dead boy is wrong,
but I keep it to myself.

I think the monster is just like
my brother and me—
lonely, longing to be loved.

The Dead Boy and the Storm
with a nod to William Stafford

I am only two,
and this is my first memory
of the dead boy.

Maple branches pound
the living room windows,
flashes of light, then boom.

My eight-year-old brother
hunkers in the corner behind
the fake gold pot that holds
the fake, giant orange tree.
Plastic leaves crown his hair.

Our parents are elsewhere.

Don't be scared,
I whisper to the dead boy,
throw my arms around his neck.

My brother doesn't answer,
just trembles.

The storm furies on.

My brother and I
stay close and quiet,
huddled together.

We remain like this
a long time,

but not

forever.

The Dead Boy As Artist

Mother needs to go to the hospital
for something called *gallstones*.
You no-good kids did this to me,
she says to my brother and me.

The dead boy runs to his room,
tears already staining his face.

I say, *No, mommy,*
I didn't throw stones at you.

Get lost, Mother shouts.
I'm sick of you.

I hide in my closet.
Only five, I have perfected
crying myself to sleep
atop a pile of too-small shoes.

A stray dog comes to visit our house
while Mother is having an operation.
My brother names the dog Ricky,
feeds him French fries.

Can we keep Ricky? I say to Daddy.
Only if your mother says okay, he answers.

The dead boy paints a picture of Ricky
so close to real, it's almost like a photo.

Daddy takes the painting as a present
when he visits Mother in the hospital.

*I didn't know you could draw
that good,* I say to my brother.

Neither did I, he says.

When mother comes home,
she finds the dog Ricky
sleeping in her bed
and doesn't scream at us.

Art is power, the dead boy tells me.
All my drawings look like fried eggs.

The Dead Boy Likes Ketchup

on eggs,
on home fries,
on toast.

On hamburgers,
on pickles,
on potato chips.

My brother even puts ketchup
on peanut butter and jelly sandwiches,
on chocolate ice cream.

Daddy says, *I should buy stock in Heinz.*
Mother yells like it's the first time,
every time the dead boy pours it on.

My brother keeps saying,
Pass me the ketchup,

until one day,
he doesn't.

I say, *Here's your ketchup.*
I even unscrew the lid for him.

No thanks, my brother says.

My mother doesn't notice.
My father turns to the sports section.

Maybe death
is like this.

The Dead Boy and Barbie

It's the 4th of July and my baby doll,
the one that says *Mama*,
has been missing for days.
My brother says, *The dog took it,
buried it somewhere.*

After sparklers, I watch the dead boy
light firecrackers in our sandpit backyard.
Get us some popsicles, my brother says.
So I go.

When I come back, I see
my Malibu Barbie duct-taped
to a red plastic box with string,
below her sit sticks of what look like
cartoon dynamite.

My brother pulls the string.
Mama, Mama, the plastic box says,
like my baby doll once did.

The dead boy lights the fuses.

I drop the popsicles.
No, I say, but no sound escapes my mouth.
Everything happens in slow motion,
like I am running through water.

In seconds, my Malibu doll
explodes in a blue cloud.
Melted bits of Barbie flesh
and red plastic and ash
rain down
all over all of us.

I am too stunned to cry,
but later, in my bedroom,
I cry for hours.

Now, I can finally laugh.
It has taken me years to appreciate
my brother's true gift—
ridding me once and for all
of that anti-feminist,
impossible-body-standard
Barbie.

The Dead Boy Likes Chocolate Best

Why it is always summer
when I am with the dead boy again?
This time, I am four going on five.

It is just before my bulimia,
another east coast humid afternoon,
a sweltering bus tour around Maine,
that makes me dizzy, motion sick.

My parents and brother go somewhere
while I lie on a bench in a parking lot.
The lady bus driver watches over me.
She says, *Your face would look pretty
on a milk carton.*
That's the nicest thing anyone's
ever told me.

Mother and Daddy return licking vanilla
ice cream cones three scoops high.
My brother carries two cones—
one chocolate, one mint chip, my favorite.

Is that one for me? I say, pointing.

You were a pain in the ass, Mother says.
Little sickie, you get shit, bupkis.
She slaps my brother on the back.

The dead boy stumbles toward
a fly-buzzing trash can,
holds the cone upside down
so my ice cream plops in.
Every last scoop.
Then, my brother drops
in the empty cone too.

The air is so hot, my tears feel cool.
Why did you throw away my cone?
I say to my brother. *I hate you.*

No hate in this family, Daddy says.
Mother says. *Good boy.*
*I told your brother to do it,
and for once, he listened.*

After the dead boy betrays me,
there is never enough
ice cream in the world,
never enough of anything
to fill me up.

The Dead Boy Tricks Me

I am six years old,
and it is one of those summer days
we will become nostalgic for—
sunshine a shade of gold
that no longer exists.

The dead boy and his friends
play with toy soldiers
in the sandpit yard
that once held a put-up pool.

I stick Goldie Locks Colorforms
on cardboard, trying hard
not to lose one of the three bears.

Happy not to be alone, I hum
Who's afraid of the big bad wolf?
a song watching Bugs Bunny taught me.

My brother says, *Hey dummy, c'mere.*
Mother calls me dummy sometimes too.
Put those soldiers in groups of three,
the dead boy says.

By color? I say, going to him,
noticing the red, green, and yellow.

My brother slaps my face.

It smarts, but not as much as
when Mother whacks me
with the dictionary.

I jam my fists over my eyes,
try to push the tears back in.

Tag-along brat, the dead boy says,
then pulls down my shorts.

My panties go down with them.

My brother's friends laugh.
Naked ass cry baby,
the dead boy says.

I hike up my pants and panties,
run for the house,
but my brother sticks out his leg
and I am face down
in doggy poo.

The dead boy asks his friends
whenever they come over
our house after this,
*Remember the day my sister
ate dog shit?*

I will never forget
the day I learned
about shame,
my brother's, my own.

Play Dead

Our dog Ricky loves everyone
except the dead boy.

My brother is always pulling
the leash too hard,
ordering our dog to play dead.

Ricky offers a paw, sits, begs.
Everything but play dead.

The dead boy yells too loud,
so our dog runs away from him,
tail tucked.

One night after we all go to bed,
the dead boy leaves Ricky outside,
then locks the door
and goes to sleep himself.

A five am phone call wakes us.
The veterinarian says
our dog was brought in,
hit by a car, crushed skull,
doesn't have long to live.

My father races to the vet
to hold Ricky as he dies.

My brother doesn't
come out of his room
until suppertime.

I imagine the dead boy
and our dead dog Ricky
are true friends now.
They play fetch in heaven.

The Dead Boy Babysits

My brother is thirteen,
a man by Jewish yardstick.
Our parents leave him in charge
of me and the cat.
Our cat runs off, hides.
I am too fat and slow to escape.

The dead boy ties me to a chair,
forces me to watch bowling
on TV for hours,
the sound turned up so high
I hear thunder in my head
the next two days.

When the show ends,
my brother lets me go.

I run from the house
into a sudden thunderstorm.
I have no coat,
so I try to get back inside.

The dead boy has locked
all the doors.

I press the bell again and again.
I pound.

My brother doesn't come.

I skulk to the backyard,
plop to the floor of the potting shed
that smells like dirt and motor oil.

Rain ticks on the roof.
There's bowling pin thunder, but maybe
it's only the sound of my own pulse.

I could go ring the neighbor's.
They would let me in, feed me,
but I want to stay quiet a while,
stay hidden, so maybe the dead boy
will worry where I am.

Maybe my brother will miss me too.

The Dead Boy Goes Hungry

My brother wiggles
his plate of meatloaf
under my nose,
says, *I fed your supper
to the dog.*

I am eight and I am starving.
I hate you,
I say to the dead boy,
and push the plate
out of his hands
into a magnificent crash.
Sauce and ceramic bits
fly everywhere.

The dead boy stares
at the red sunburst mess
spread across yellow linoleum.
Sweat beads his forehead.

You're nobody, nothing,
I say to my brother.

The moment these
words leave my lips
I am a different person,
a terrible human being,
a worthless sister.

The dead boy's
entire body shakes.
Tears stream down
his cheeks.

My eyes remain dry.
Until now.

Rare Photo of the Dead Boy

There's a wood-paneled wall behind
my brother and me.

My skin is the color of caramel
and I'm wearing a red sleeveless top,
so it must be summer.

My hair is pulled back tight
in an elastic, Mother's constant
effort to deny my afro.

The dead boy's long hair
hangs down in straight, greasy blades.
His cheeks and nose are sunburnt rose.
He looks all of sixteen.

I stare directly into the camera,
but point to my brother.
The dead boy's pointing at me too.

We look silly, have identical
buck-toothed smiles.

I never noticed how
alike we are smiling.
In our family, we almost never smile,
and never ever at the same time.

For at least the second it took
to snap this Polaroid,
something made my brother
and me happy.

I wish to God I knew what it was,
and that it lasted as long
as the photo.

The Dead Boy Relaxes

My brother has a twitchy leg.

Me, I like to eat.
If my mouth is chewing,
I don't feel much of anything.

The dead boy's leg relaxes
only when he's penning
comic strips using India ink.

The dead boy's friends say
he's gonna be famous someday.

But when the art school recruiter
comes to our house,
my brother yells at him to
Get the hell out.

The dead boy studies
electrical engineering instead,
gets a job making nuclear bombs
communicate better.

He stops drawing altogether
and his leg never calms.

The Dead Boy Is Mugged

I am nine years old
and have been practicing
being the good child
for many years.

Still, Mother says to me,
for forgetting to set the table,
You're an ignoramus.
I'm not sure what it means,
but it sounds terrible.

My brother is a teenager,
practicing not caring
what any adult says.

One day, the dead boy arrives
home for supper later than usual.
His cheeks are dirty, streaked,
his polo shirt torn,
blood caked on his elbows.

What the hell happened to you?
Mother says.

I got jumped, my brother says,
his face is a balloon
about to burst.
Two f*ckers stole my bike.

Serves you right, Mother says.
*I told you not to go near the weeds.
You can forget about us buying you
a bike or anything else, ever again.*

The weeds is the swampy place
between Queens and Brooklyn
where there's nothing but
a field full of broken beer bottles.
People say drug dealers
hang out there and girls get raped.

Mother says, *You are a stupid
piece of shit, you know that?*
She could be talking to either of us.

I spy a pack of *Kools* peeking out
from the dead boy's back pocket.
I go hug him, scrunch down
the cigarette pack
so Mother doesn't notice.
I figure he's in enough trouble.

My brother throws an arm around me
in a half-hug, mouths the word, *thanks*.

Mother says, *I wish you'd
died in the womb.*
She's said that to me before, too.

The dead boy's tears flow
like an open facet.
He's no good
at ignoring our mother.

My brother will never completely
shut out our Mother's hateful words,
no matter how much he practices.

The Dead Boy Cruises

This may be the happiest
moment of my life.
I never get to tag along
with my brother at nighttime.

I'm in the backseat
of the dead boy's
hilarious friend Vinnie's
red AMC Pacer,
squeezed into the middle hump
by his friends,
Richard (the smart one)
and Danny (the cute one).
My brother rides shotgun.

The windows rolled down,
the stars clear,
the radio throngs
"The Night Chicago Died"
all the way up
Rockaway Boulevard.

Everyone is quiet.
All there is
is the cruise,
and the breeze,
and song after song,
that make my heart beat
likes it's in my throat.

As if to signal a turn,
the dead boy
extends his arm
out the open window.
My brother's hand becomes
a sail.

THE DEAD BOY GETS ENGAGED

which is a very strange thing
for my brother who never phoned a girl,
never had a girl phone him,
never seemed to go out on dates.

I guess he's better at secrets than I am.

Stranger still, the girl is smart,
good-looking, and talkative.
Maybe the dead boy won't
relive our family trauma as Freud says
we're all doomed to do.

The girl tells us they met on a blind date,
and she knew right away
my brother was *the one*.

Me, I'm dating a rebound guy
after getting dumped
for the umpteenth time
for someone skinnier, prettier.

Turns out my boyfriend is made
in the image of Mother,
will try to strangle me
two weeks into our marriage
when I sober up and he doesn't.

Today, the dead boy is beaming.
He's speaking more than he has
all his years in this house.

We all gather around
the dining room table
to eat deli sandwiches and potato salad

in celebration of their engagement,
like this is all perfectly normal,
like real people might do,
or at least, like the families
we see on TV.

The Dead Boy's Father Dies

Our father is fond of
Hershey bars
and knock-knock jokes.
Strange dogs love him
and our father loves
my brother and me,
but it is like being loved
from far away,
a place where the weather
is always hazy.

When Daddy dies of lung cancer
metastasized to brain cancer,
Mother says to the dead boy,
*Your father was disappointed
in you, furious you weren't
a better son to us.*

My brother's eyes are lit coals.

That's not true, I tell the dead boy
*Don't listen to her.
Daddy didn't talk that way.
He always said he was proud of you.*

Later, at the *shiva*
at my brother's house,
our shy little cousin
won't say hello to the dead boy.

My brother's eyes stare past the cousin,
stare past me, bore into a wall.

I close my own eyes,
but even from inside my eyelids,
I am aware that we live in a country
at war with itself,
all hope of truce lost.

THE DEAD BOY BECOMES A FATHER

It is a yellow spring day
that smells like rubber
and pond frogs.

The news arrives by phone call—
the dead boy and his wife
have a newborn son.

Into the receiver,
I tell my brother,
wanting to believe it,
I'm so happy for you.

What I want to say
and don't is,

*Please, please, please,
do exactly the opposite
of what our parents did.*

The Dead Boy Saves Lives

It starts with him manning
a ham radio for the Red Cross,
but now the dead boy wants
to save lives,
so he becomes
a volunteer EMT.

He can't put it into words,
but talks about blood gasses.

At a special training session on 9/11,
Word Trade Center building #4,
my brother is front and center
for tragedy.

The dead boy sees women
kick off heels to run—
one darts in front of a taxi,
dies before his eyes.

My brother does all he can,
helps save life after life,
then walks across the boroughs until
he finally arrives home safe, but exhausted.

On the phone, the dead boy says
At first, we thought it was bombs,
people panicked,
women kicked off heels to run,
one headed straight into traffic,
was mowed down by a taxi.

My brother is silent a moment,
then there's a catch in his breath,
I just wish I could have done more.

The Dead Boy Shrinks

My brother receives chemo treatments.
After six weeks, he's released
from the hospital, his white cell
blood count acceptable for visitors.

I come thousands of miles to see him,
pause on the front porch a moment
before I can ring the bell,
afraid I won't say the right thing.

The dead boy answers the door.
You're here, he says.
We thought you got lost.

*A long line at the car rental
place,* I explain.

My brother's head is bald
as a baby's, his face missing
brows and lashes.
He's pale and frail.

I realize we are seeing
eye to eye—
his like hard-boiled eggs—
equal height,
though the dead boy used to be
taller than me.

*Still can't be too careful
about germs,* my brother says.
So don't kiss me.

I am ashamed to admit
it never occurs to me
to kiss the dead boy.

The Dead Boy Enlists

I lose count
how many treatments
my brother has taken,
some large number
of experimental
chemo cocktails.

The leukemia lessens,
regains,
lessens,
regains.

The dead boy learns
kindness
at the hands of
strangers in white.

Good to see you,
my brother says
when I come to visit
him in the hospital.

His voice cracks
like when he was going
through puberty.
I am fighting the good fight.

Being a Conservative Jew,
the dead boy doesn't see the irony
in his uttering the credo
of Christian missionaries.

I say, *Stay positive,*
even though I know
miracles happen only
to Jesus believers.

The Dead Boy Inspires Me to Ice

When it becomes clear
my brother will not overcome
his illness,
I travel north.

So far north, ice there
is hundreds and hundreds
of years old.

Something as simple
as frozen water
will outlast the dead boy,
will outlast me,
even when I become
the dead girl.

The ice in my glass
of iced tea
melts in under an hour.

Imagine it,
dear dying, not-yet
dead boy brother,
fields of fjords older than
any living being on earth.

I go north to touch a glacier,
to hold the glacier's blue-glaze
calf in my hand.

I handle this cold gift of time
none of us are given.

I need this glacier
to know
something lasts.

That one plain thing
goes on
and on,
even though
it should not
be possible.

A Mitzvah For the Dead Boy

It has been a year in the plans,
big as a wedding,
complete with a smoke mirage,
and a troupe of rabbis who boogie
with wine bottles on their head,
the Bar Mitzvah
for my brother's oldest son.

My brother smiles more this day
than his entire life.
Such a mitzvah

My nephew sings the Lord's word,
later plays drums to The Beatles'
"I Wanna Hold Your Hand."
This child turned man,
his father's greatest pride.

My brother doesn't wear
the prescribed hygienic gloves,
allows everyone to shake his hand,
offers hugs.

A month from now
my brother will be dead,
but for tonight
the dead boy dances
and dances.

A Mother's Day Gift For the Dead Boy

It's Mother's Day weekend.
I'm in New York visiting Mother
at the nursing home.

I dial the hospital room
where my brother's
been worsening for weeks.

In just a few days from now,
I will fly back to New York again
to tell our mother
her son is gone.

She will say to me,
The wrong child died.
It should have been you.

But right now,
Mother says over the phone,
I want you to be well.
She tells my brother,
I love you.

And I realize I was mistaken—
miracles
can happen to Jews.

The Dead Boy's Last Words to Me

It is May.
My brother stares
into the flat silver light
outside his hospital room window.

The dead boy is well enough
to walk with a walker,
so we trudge to the elevator
and back around, his gown
flapping open behind him.
My brother is beyond shame now.

I grasp his bird-bone wrist
as if he might fly away.

His eyes protrude
like a sad Chihuahua's,
but the dead boy is cheerful.

Look at those great flowers,
he says as we pass several bouquets
parked at the nurses' station.
People don't realize, he says,
*patients here are too sick
to have blooms in their rooms.*

What I think and do not say is,
Save those flowers for the grave.

So many things
I want to ask my brother,
but I don't want to impose
on his strength, upset his mood.

When we get back to his room,
the dead boy is exhausted.
I have to go, I say.
My flight's in a few hours.

Thanks for coming,
my brother says.

I love you, I say.

I love you,
the dead boy says.

Every time we part now,
we say this,
after a lifetime
of never finding the words.

This will be the last time.

Tonight, after I board the plane
for the west coast, my brother
will slip into a coma.

When I am in the air
watching city lights disappear,
I realize the best part,
the worst part,
of *I love you*
is truly meaning it.

The Dead Boy Teaches Me About Impermanence

Do the dead age?
If so, my brother, the dead boy,
is fifty-four now in heaven,
or the ether,
or the coffin,
or nowhere at all.

I'm older now than my brother ever was.
The dead boy had more to live for than me,
with his loving wife and two young sons.
I should have traded my days for his sleep.

I keep thinking I've reached the age
where someone I love
will die every year,
and time proves me right.
My best friend dies of a brain tumor.
My poetry mentor dies on my birthday.

When it's my turn,
I hope to die with as much
grace as my brother
who on his last conscious day
with a clear, unbroken voice
said, *I'm satisfied we did everything*
we could do,
but it just isn't enough.

The dead boy spent his days
in between hospital stays
getting his house in order—
fixing leaks,
re-carpeting the basement
upgrading the computers.

My brother did what he could
for his family and nothing for himself.
I wanted to ask him what
his last wish was,
but somehow, I forgot.

I want to ask the dead boy
what made him decide years before
becoming so ill
to stop making bombs better,
to work on railroad trains instead,
and start saving lives as an EMT,
but I will never get the chance.

So now, I ask the air about epiphany,
hoping my brother
can hear me, somehow.
I wish he'd come visit me
in a dream,
tell me how to stop grieving.

It has been a cold wet spring,
but finally there are blooms
and a day warm enough
to go coatless a few hours.

I am near the sea
remembering another day long,
long ago when the dead boy spent hours
building an elaborate sand castle
with only a few Dixie cups
and a popsicle stick
to design his creation.

He constructed turrets and towers
Cinderella would covet.
Finished, my brother stepped back
to appraise his work.

Take a last look, the dead boy said,
then threw himself upon the grand mansion,
flapping his arms, flailing his legs,
utterly annihilating the sand castle.

Why? was the only thing
I managed to say.

Why not? my brother said,
a sly smile filling his eyes.
Nothing lasts forever,
not even time.

The Dead Boy's Eyes Radiate Light

Go see the redwoods,
my brother says.
Treat yourself
for your birthday.
He bounces on one leg,
like always.

I've wanted to go there
my whole life, I say.

I know, so go, the dead boy says,
bathed in the morning shade
of a Japanese maple
at my Puget Sound home
he's never visited before.

We moved out to Seattle
before he got so ill.

But my brother looks fine,
no sign whatsoever
of leukemia's ravages.

The dead boy's eyes shine
as if lit from within.

I remember Red Cross officers
wearing dress blues,
saluting your casket,
I say. *So this is a dream.*

True, my brother says,
but that doesn't make
our time together
any less real.

The Dead Boy Visits the Hayden Planetarium

which surprises me because
my brother's funeral
was just a few days ago.

Tonight he is here for
The Beatles Laser Light Show
and so am I,
and we are both alone.

He sits a few rows ahead of me.
I won't realize it
in the psychedelic bliss
until the show ends with
"Let it Be"
and the house lights come on.

The dead boy's hair
is back to its slick black fullness,
his skin, blush again.

Hello, I call.

You are here too,
my brother says,
as if it is nothing
to meet like this
in a dream of Manhattan.

Are you well? I say.
But the dead boy ignores
my question.

*I remember I saw this show
thirty years ago,*

he says.
*Thought I'd see it again
one last time.*

*How about we go get
some coffee?* I say.

No. It's late, my brother says.
I have to get back.

Back where? I say,
not wanting the real answer.

The dead boy shakes his head,
half-laughs, half-coughs,
then steps out the door,
outside the planetarium
to the stone walkway

where I know
he's already become
moonlight.

Godzilla and The Dead Boy's Doppelganger

Dear dead brother,
I can never see the actor
Matthew Broderick
without seeing your
forehead, nose, ears, hair
and overall stature.

I can never see Godzilla without
recalling endless
bowls of Captain Crunch
all those Saturday mornings
when Mother was at the beauty parlor
getting dye-and-doed
and Daddy mowed the lawn
(a ten by ten square that took hours),
or else fussed with wrenches
to fix who knows what,

while you and I watched
Japanese monster movies
because you were older and stronger,
took control over the TV,
and that's what you wanted to watch.

All that screeching,
all those explosions,
all those cities getting destroyed,
nothing like the real thing
in lower Manhattan
that turns you into the dead boy.

Godzilla, Mothra,
bigger than we thought our lives
ever could be,

even on the tiny screen
of a black & white.

Rodan, King Ghidorah,
for those noisy ninety minutes,
badder than any trouble
Mother could throw our way.

Now, you are dead almost a year
and it's a rainy Saturday morning.
I lay drowsy on the couch
flipping through channels
to find a Godzilla remake
starring Matthew Broderick.

It's Matthew Broderick
as my brother the hero,
and for these ninety minutes
you aren't the dead boy any more,

and you are more than
the hero of New York City.
You are the hero
of your own life
and of mine too.

Dear brother,
you are the hero
of all the mutant,
misunderstood
monsters—
especially those
we call
family.

About the Author

Lana Hechtman Ayers is a poetry publisher, movie addict, and time travel enthusiast. She facilitates Write Away™ generative writing workshops, leads private salons for book groups, and teaches at writers' conferences. She is obsessed with exotic flavors of ice cream, Little Red Riding Hood, and monochromatic cats and dogs.

Lana is a Hedgebrook alumna. She holds an MFA in Writing Popular Fiction and an MFA in Poetry, as well as degrees in Psychology and Mathematics. She's previously authored eight collections of poetry, and is at work on several speculative novels.

In addition to thriving in the book-loving culture, she enjoys the Pacific Northwest's bountiful rain and copious coffee shops. Her favorite color is the swirl of Van Gogh's *Starry Night*.

Visit Lana online at LanaAyers.com.

www.ingramcontent.com/pod-product-compliance
Lightning Source LLC
Chambersburg PA
CBHW020618300426
44113CB00007B/697